Earth
Water
Air
Fire
Spirit

p o e m s

j. bruce jones

brucejonesdesign.com

EARTH

WATER

AIR

FIRE

SPIRIT

Published by Bruce Jones Design

781-492-0742 • https://www.BruceJonesDesign.com

Amazon Author Central Page
http://www.amazon.com/author/jbrucejones

EARTH

BLUE AND SECURE

Our home blue and secure
Turning towards the sun
We climb to the heavens
With the swirl of the sky
Peace brings unto us

FIELD MIST

The light of dawn
Across the fields
With mist below my feet
I reach for the clouds
With goals so deep

MOUNTAIN TOPS

The weight of the mountains
Is felt in our souls
Snow tops bringing us comfort
Grey to white is but air to earth
We are higher as we breath lower

ANCIENT SPIRITS

Ancient spirits lock us to the earth
Steady around the stars
We align to our soul
Breath to our beings
And listen to our hearts

SUN AND STARS

From earth to light
We grow anew each day
The struggle to climb
To the sun and stars
One being across another

COLD NIGHTS

The whisper of light touches us
Nature runs with deep breaths
The earth lifts up to the sky
On cold winter nights
We wrap her in our life

WATER

ENERGY RIPPLES

The power of energy
Crests around us
Mist breaks from the edge
Rhythm of life ripples
Bringing us closer

PATTERN OF THE DAY

Red in the pattern of the day
Light falls to water
We burst to the clouds
As the soul emerges
Take as you are given

CROSSING WAVES

Yes, it is time
To break the bonds of flow
Drop gently down
To new crossing waves
Color and life will emerge

LINE OF LIGHT

Peaceful break of waves
Brings a reach of greater depths
The line of light
Anchors to new horizons
Rippling out from the center

MOUNTAIN REFLECTIONS

Reflections of sky to earth
Broken with light across the water
Float gently together
We follow the path
Mountains up, look left

WINGS TOUCHING

Line of flight across the sky
Beneath the clouds
We follow with wings touching
Gentle waves mimic
Our movement below

AIR

QUIET WHISPER

Quiet, we all stop
As light brings forth joy
Climb above your heart
With mist to reflect
Whisper across the dark

SPRING LIFE

Reach each one
In stillness and love
Holding for spring
The inner grasp
Of life to come

MYSTERY SKY

Wind blows across the sky
Movement pushes back
We learn as one
And work to find
A way above the mystery

GENTLE SKY

Gentle, delicate, fragile
Life springs forth in pattern
Uniqueness we are one
Spreading across the sky
To touch and renew

NEW IDEAS

Through the mass of air
We breath in new life
We stand in new hope
We cross new ideas
Let us rise up and flow

SHALLOW DARKNESS

Above we know not below
What movement go there
Strength is shallow
When darkness closes
Soar to live again

FIRE

NURTURE THE PATH

The heat of life breaths with energy
Red flames nurture the path
As we move across
Bring it back
To where it passes

OUR JOURNEY

Radiant light silhouettes the dark
Under the near day
Reminding us of our journey
To before our path
We must find

LIGHTED PATH

Light sparkles against the touch
Bright then falls
Our energy is certain
As we struggle to fine
A path through

LOVE IS DEEP

A single light of our soul
Climbs and wavers
Heat is instant
As love secures
Our ability to deep

WARM AND COMFORT

One by one we support
The warmth of old
Together it comforts
And drops the by
For we have the renew

REFLECTION IN PEACE

Simple we support
As we reflect in peace
Flames of life around each
Come again we join
And start for this one

SPIRIT

OUR SOULS CLIMB

Sky above with touch
Bring my love to below
I reckon your breath
Pierces my soul
I reach and climb with you

HEART TO BREATH

In peace is sleep
Ancient passes through
I close and breath
My heart to you
One day more

REACHING BEYOND

We pull far from center
With focus so near
Break the bonds
That hold us dear
Reach beyond

FALL INTO SOLITUDE

Lean we fall
Whisper to the trees
In spirit repeated
We emerge to light
With solitude and breath

SOULS SLIP QUIETLY

From behind we emerge
To feather across divide
Reflection of the soul
Slips quietly down
And in we come

SPRING RENEWS

Peace with gratitude
In spring the release
Of life from before
And through to now
With love and quiet understanding

J. Bruce Jones
is a Mystic, CT author and designer.

EARTH
WATER
AIR
FIRE
SPIRIT

poems

j. bruce jones

brucejonesdesign.com